to Arvida Steen

TEN FOLK CAROLS FOR CHRISTMAS

from the United States

Jane Frazee

STAP022

SCHOTT

London · Mainz · New York · Tokyo

STAP022

© 1977 Schott Music Corporation

ISBN 0 930448 02 2

TABLE OF CONTENTS

INTRODUCTION

This collection of American folk carols offers examples of both the religious and festive celebrations of Christmas. The songs are simple in construction and accessible in range. The supporting instrumental parts, built on ostinati and drone accompaniment figures, have been especially developed to complement the voice and recorder parts. Any necessary substitutions should be made with careful considerations of register and color.

These little pieces speak to children of all ages, so direct and forthright is their expression of the human response to the miracle of Christmas.

Jane Frazee
Minneapolis, 1977

SOURCES

1. Look Away to Bethlehem: From an 1880 collection entitled
   Revival Hymns and Plantation Melodies
2. Oh Watch the Stars: St. Helena Island, South Carolina
3. Shine Like a Star in the Morning: Archive of American
   Folksong, Library of Congress
4. Cradle Hymn: Tennessee
5. See Jesus the Saviour: Kentucky
6. Old Christmas: Kentucky Fiddle Tune
7. Jesus, Jesus Rest Your Head: Kentucky
8. Wasn't That a Mighty Day: St. Helena Island, South Carolina
9. Sing All Men: Kentucky
10. Jesus the Christ is Born: Tennessee

ABBREVIATIONS

Soprano Glockenspiel	SG
Alto Glockenspiel	AG
Soprano Xylophone	SX
Alto Xylophone	AX
Bass Xylophone	BX
Alto Metallophone	AM
Bass Metallophone	BM
Hand drum	HD
Tambourine	Tamb
Wood block	WB
Claves	CL
Maracas	Mar
Triangle	TR
Cymbals	C
Finger Cymbals	FC
Voice(s)	V
Soprano Recorder	Sopr. R
Alto Recorder	Alto R

1. Look Away to Bethlehem

2. Oh Watch the Stars

Oh watch the stars, see how they run,_____ Oh watch the stars, see how they run,_____ The stars come

out_____ at the setting of the sun, _____ Oh watch the stars, See how they run._____

3. Shine Like a Star in the Morning

Shine,_____ shine, Shine_ like a_ star in the morn-ing,__

Shine,_____ shine, all a-round the throne of God, God knows I'm going to God.

4. Cradle Hymn

Hush, my babe, lie still and slum - ber, Ho - ly an - gels guard thy bed,

9

5. See Jesus the Saviour

shel - ter for Ma - ry, who Je - sus did car - ry, Ah _ _ _ _ _ _ _ _ _ _ _ _ _ _ 2. See

Je - sus the Sav - iour a - sleep in the man - ger, - Ah _ _ _ _ _ _ _ _

11

Fath - er on high look'd down from the sky, Ah —

Ah —

6. Old Christmas

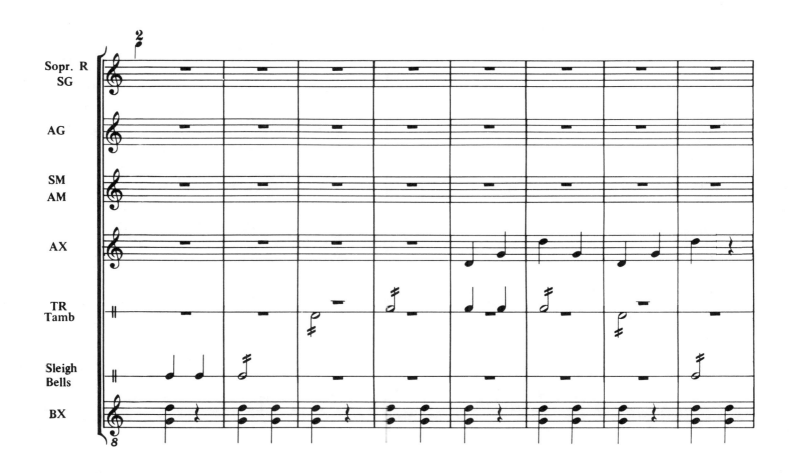

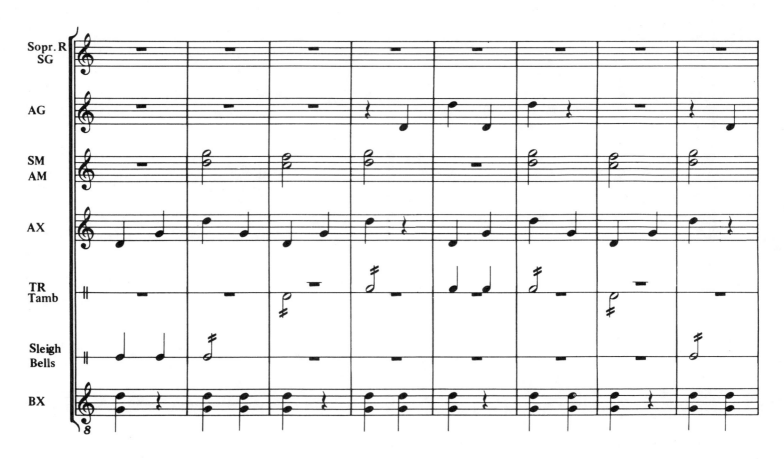

14

(Add voices on "la")

7. Jesus, Jesus, Rest Your Head

Je - sus, Je - sus, rest your head, You has got a man - ger bed,

All the e - vil folk on earth, Sleep in fea - thers at their_ birth,

Je - sus, Je - sus, rest your head, You has got a man - ger bed.

8. Wasn't That a Mighty Day

Wasn't that a migh - ty day, Hal - le - lu, ⸺ Hal - le - lu, ⸺

Wasn't that a migh - ty day, When Je - sus Christ was born. Well,

9. Sing, All Men!

1. Sing all men 'tis Christ-mas morn-ing, Je-sus Christ the Son's a-born-ing,

Chorus, Verses 1 and 2

Heigh, the hol-ly! Ho, the hea-ther Car-ol voi-ces all to-geth-er!

*With Mallet

2. In that manger all alone,
   The Virgin Mother did atone.

3. He who came to earth so low
   Soon to man's estate will grow.

Chorus, Verse 3

Heigh the hol - ly! Ho, the hea - ther! Car - ol voi - ces all to - geth - er!

Heigh the hol - ly! Ho, the hea - ther! Car - ol voi - ces all to - geth - er!

* With Mallet

10. Jesus the Christ is Born

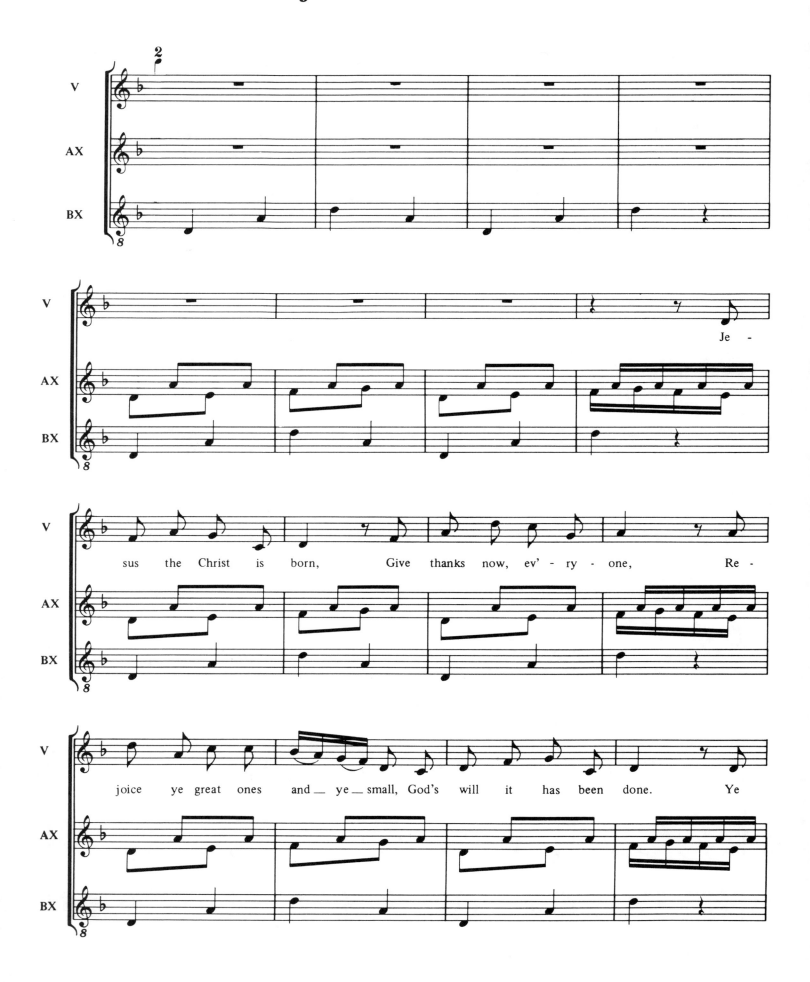

24